You are not only my

_____, but also

my _____

1

Love consists of this: two solitudes that meet, protect and greet each other.

-Rainer Maria Rilke

Whenever I am around
you I feel _____

Love is like the wind, you can't see it,
but you can feel it.

-Nicholas Sparks

It means the world to me
when you _____

Love doesn't make the world go round.
Love is what makes the ride worthwhile.

-Franklin P. Jones

Just being around
you makes me feel

All you need is love. But a little chocolate now and then doesn't hurt.

-Charles Schulz

Two of my favorite
moments from the past year
with you were

_____

_____

It is better to love wisely, no doubt: but to love foolishly is better than not to be able to love at all.

-William Thackeray

You make my heart

_____

Love is a smoke and is made with the fume of sighs.

-Shakespeare

I love you as much as the

_____ is

_____

Love is the answer to everything.
It's the only reason to do anything.
If you don't write stories you love,
you'll never make it. If you don't write
stories that other people love,
you'll never make it.

-Ray Bradbury

Whenever you

_____

my

_____

I just can't

_____

The opposite of love is not hate;

it's indifference.

-Elie Wiesel

I really want to

_____ you in the

_____ for the rest

of our lives

Love is something sent from Heaven to worry the Hell out of you.

-Dolly Parton

There is something I've been meaning to tell you —

_____

_____

Passion makes the world go round.
Loves just makes it a safer place.

-Ice T

I want you to know that from
the bottom of my heart,

_____

_____

Love is a promise; love is a souvenir, once given never forgotten, never let it disappear.

-John Lennon

I'll never forget the first
time we _____

_____

Love is composed of a single soul
inhabiting two bodies.

-Aristotle

The first time I met you
I felt

_____

_____

Love is of all passions the strongest,
for it attacks simultaneously the head,
the heart, and the senses.

-Lau Tzu

I really appreciate you
putting up with all my

_____

_____

In dreams and in love,
there a no impossibilities.

- Janos Arnay

I love it when you

There is no remedy for love
but to love more.

-Henry David Thoreau

Your
_____

makes me want to
_____

Love is a serious mental disease.

-Plato

I've never told you,
but I love it when you

_____

Love is the hardest habit to break

and the most difficult to satisfy.

-Drew Barrymore

I want to

_____

With you

Love is a game that two can play
and both win.

-Eva Gabor

I will always love you
despite the fact you

We're born alone, we live alone, we die alone. Only through our love and friendship can we create the illusion for the moment that we're not alone.

-Orson Wells

Your

makes me want to jump for joy

Love is the greatest refreshment in life.

-Pablo Picasso

Your _____

makes me want to hide

under the covers

Love always brings difficulties,
that is true, but the good side
of it is that it gives energy.

-Vincent Van Gogh

Life is more

With you in it. Please

Love involves a peculiar unfathomable combination of understanding and misunderstanding.

-Diane Arbus

I will take you on a trip to

_____

and feed you

_____

under the

_____

Absence sharpens love, presence strengthens it.

-Benjamin Franklin

If my heart could speak English, it would say

47

Love never claims, it ever gives.
Love ever suffers, never resents never

revenges itself.

-Gandhi

When I say

I mean every word of it

Darkness cannot drive out darkness:
only light can do that. Hate cannot
drive out hate: only love can do that.

-Martin Luther King, Jr.

The first time I saw you
there was something

_____

about you. Maybe it was
the way you

_____

Whatever our souls are made of, his and
mine are the same.
- Wuthering Heights

I love the way you

_____ when you

_____

Death cannot stop true love. All it can do is delay it for a while.

-The Princess Bride

I couldn't imagine
my life without your

_____

Love is an emotion experienced by the many and enjoyed by the few.

-Unknown

I will never forget the time

we _____

Love without reason lasts the longest.

-Unknown

_____ was the

moment I knew I loved you

Never love anybody who treats you like
you're ordinary.

-Oscar Wilde

One last thing

_____

_____

_____

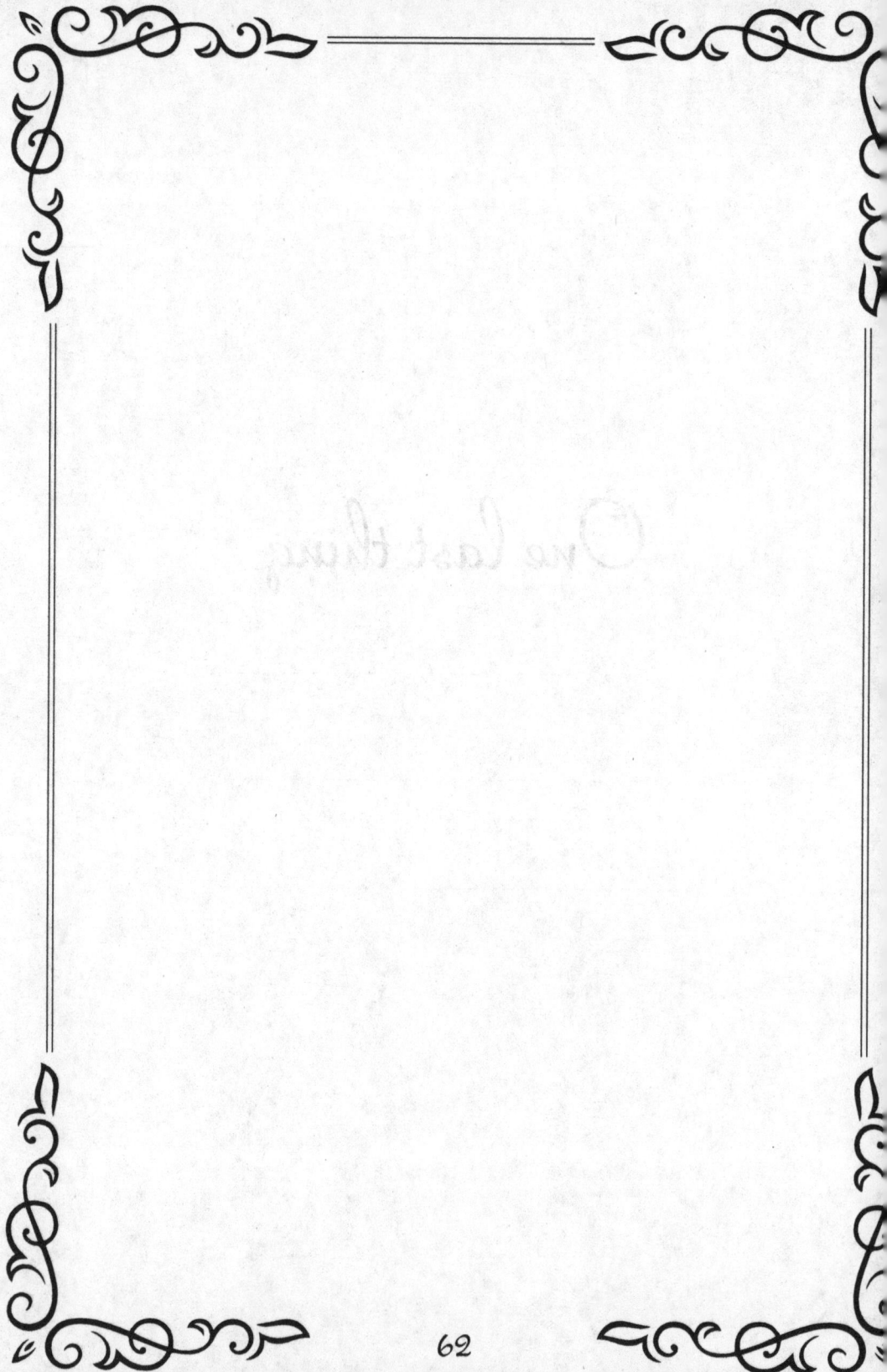

www.ingramcontent.com/pod-product-compliance
Lightning Source LLC
Chambersburg PA
CBHW011338290326
41933CB00046B/3456